MEXICO

A Play

by

GERTRUDE STEIN

GREEN INTEGER
KOBENHAVEN & LOS ANGELES
1999

GREEN INTEGER
Edited by Per Bregne
København/Los Angeles

Distributed in the United States
by Consortium Book Sales and Distribution,
1045 Westgate Drive, Suite 90
Saint Paul, Minnesota 55114-1065

This book was published in collaboration with
The Contemporary Arts Educational Project, Inc, a non-profit corporation,
through a matching grant from the National Endowment for the Arts,
a federal agency.

NATIONAL
ENDOWMENT
FOR THE
ARTS

Design: Per Bregne
Typography: Guy Bennett

LIBRARY OF CONGRESS CATALOGING IN PUBLICATION DATA
Stein, Gertrude [1874–1946]
Mexico. A Play
ISBN: 1-892295-36-9
p. cm — Green Integer 42
I. Title II. Series

Ernestine.

Have you mentioned tracing out California.

I have.

How big is it.

As big as a boat.

What boat.

The city of Savannah.

Have you succeeded in tracing the origin of the word ugly.

I have.

It means crab.

It certainly means crab.

Crabbed is an instance.

We learn about rocking chairs from them.

Kites are an example.

We learn about peaches from them.

They learned them too.

Were you dreaming badly. No. Then go to sleep again little sweetheart.

Ernestine.

It is easy to see four boats. Boats are a ship. There are English and Danish and other boats. It is hard to tell the Italian flag. Hard almost impossible.

I do not mean to be discourteous.

Ernestine.

Come in.

John.

Did you meet him.

I did and I believed in him.

Did you go away.

No I stayed a long time.

Did you go to another country to earn your own living.

I did not I stayed here for some time.

I am going away.

I have finished everything.

I will expect a selection.

I have dreams of women.

6

Do dream of me.

I will come to see weather.

I understand what they mean by dirty weather. It's the color.

Act so that you will be spared the necessity of deceiving anyone.

I do.

I will.

They were willing to have table and bed linen and neglect dressing. They were willing to have excellent eating. They did not care about coffee.

Sarah.

Wood is not to be neglected. I will attend to everything. If he hasn't them send us his name.

What do we do with methods and respect.

Methods and respect serve us for imitation. We imitate pronunciation. Mexico.

Henry Irving.

Neglect me and believe me and caress me.

Say I am careful.

Believe in punishments. Search for many.

Many men are necessary. We are necessary. We mean more and we have faithful truths.

Mexico.

I was so pleased.

8

ACT II.

A grand opening and many boats. I like them with white sails. I like them to use better coal.

Appreciations.

Mrs. Guilbert.
I understand Welsh.
So do I.
Mrs. Hendry.
I have never been married.
I have.

Mexico.

Mexico is prettily pronounced in Spanish.
Pronounce it for me.
Yes I will.

Say it prettily.

Mexico.

There are many ways of winning a lottery.

Newspaper notoriety.

A grocery store.

A butcher shop.

A silk seller.

Embroidery.

Clothes.

Muffs.

And corduroy.

This is the way we win.

We refuse to go to theater not because we don't like it but because we'd rather go to Penfolds. Penfolds have not a pleasant house we are going there for tea tomorrow.

Mrs. Guilbert.

She has remarkable lace. She teaches English.

We have chosen a handkerchief.

William Guilbert.

He is very young. He has been here altogether. He is not older than Allan.

How old is Allan.

I do not know I think he is seventeen.

Fairly reorganized they are loading from one boat into another.

I have my foot.

Genevieve.

I do not mean to know her.

Yes you do.

I mean I have not met her.

Well that's possible.

Madeleine.

My name is Victoria.

Yes the Captain told me.

We do not address him.

He speaks English.

Yes of course he does.

Why of course we do.

We are going to begin.

Listen to one another.

We are all together.

This is a song.

Mrs. Childs.

I am decided we must not expose ourselves to the cold.

Thank you very much.

ACT III.

Now let us understand each other. We have more time than we had. Let us begin now.

A cab stand.

Who is restless.

We all are not we are not willing to go.

Very well do not go.

If there are many of you I will ask another.

He agreed to go.

He was very pleased.

I knew he would be content.

It was a mistake we should not have come at that hour.

We have to come when we can.

Quite right.

This is the right city of Mexico.

Or street of Mexico.

Street of Mexico.

Mark Guilbert.

Yes sir.

It's only a habit.

What is only a habit.

To read the autobiography of Edward Lincoln.

Who is he.

He is the man that recognized the principle of two ships.

Which two.

The Bolton and the Meadow.

Are they both here.

They are.

What are they doing.

They are taking off cargo.

Are they removing it from one ship to the other.

They are.

Genevieve.

I saw a wedding today.

The bride was dressed in black. Her veil was black.

That is because she was a widow.

Oh is that so.

What is the custom in your country.

In my country they always wear white veils.

Even widows.

Yes but unless you are rich you have a black dress.

Yes that is more economical.

And useful.

Yes certainly.

At twelve o'clock.

The fifth and sixth and seventh of January.

Fair fat and a hundred and twenty.

I was right.

Mark Guilbert.

I am free on Wednesday.

With whom do you talk.

I can do that easily.

Of course you can we wish to compliment you.

I am pleased to hear it.

SCENE III.

A play. Mexico.

This evening he mentioned that they were neglected and that they were easily disturbed.

I can understand that.

Mark Guilbert.

Do you know Bird.

No I do not that is to say I have met him and
knew about him.

He is very interesting.

A little Mexico.

Do say.

What.

When you have your teeth fixed you use rubber.

Do you.

Yes all the dentists do.

How do you manage it.

Very easily.

And very successful.

Yes indeed.

We have been singularly fortunate with electricity. It was only in the beginning that we were afraid of thunderstorms.

A little kindness.

We do not wish to invite them. When they come they ask pleasant questions.

Who is a watcher.

We are.

In that case do not forget the clock.

And a note.

And a drawing.

And you had better leave me some writing.

Do you mean to do.

No.

Very well then.

Flowers are pretty.

So are fruits.

So are meats.

So are sugars.

So are cheeses.

I like a joke about cheese.

Gilbert Ferdinand.

Why do you make a noise.

Because we are isolated.

Have you not a watchman.

Certainly sir.

First second third and fourth bird.

Do you like it.

All the time.

There is no use asking me that. We never expected
to ask any one for flowers.

That is perfectly natural.

Of course it's perfectly natural.

When you settle.

You settle with

Him.

Do you care to do it.

You care to do it if you are visited.

Everybody is visited on an island.

Ermine.

What is influence.

Influence is the pleasure some have in reminding us of villages.

Herbert.

Are villages near a city.

Not if you use the word correctly. Villages are the country. To go to a village is to leave a city.

Augustine.

Is that her name.

It is.

Why does she speak of her employer.

Because she is a servant and cooks.

Does she cook well.

Very well.

Mr. Standish.

What do you say.

You are pleased with the weather.

Yes I am pleased with the weather.

We were agreed that we would not be angry.

Mr. Murchison.

How often have I been mistaken.

You were mistaken about the length of time that foreigners would stay on the island.

Yes indeed I was.

And can anybody be obedient.

Yes it is not difficult.

Were we mistaken about the president.

Yes we were in a fashion of speaking.

How did we know.

By becoming aware of some facts with which we had not been acquainted.

Yes that is correct.

We do not need to be careful.

No indeed.

Mrs. Giles.

Why do you not state the difference between steps and road.

I have often.

What is it then.

The difference between steps and road is that one is disagreeable and the other isn't.

Certainly.

We have often noticed it.

Now we avoid the steps.

So do we.

Yes I find it is the common practice.

The steps are steep.

So is the road.

Indeed it is.

Why are you late.

I am not very late.

No you are not very late.

We have often met before.

Indeed we have.

Henrietta Fountain.

Dear me have you been here before.

Yes and seen the almonds in flower.

Yes certainly every day.

Yes indeed and with great pleasure.

Yes and some pleasure in exercise.

Yes in exercise and variety.

Yes in that continually.

Yes in that very much.

Did you happen to hear of the city of Georgia.

I did not know there existed a city of that name.

I had reference to a steamer.

Then I can certainly agree with you.

I hoped you could.

It will be a pleasure to meet again.

ACT V.

SCENE VI.

A great many plays are better than another.

Gilbert.

Come in.

Henry.

Do come in.

Francis.

A great many people come in.

Philip.

Do a great many people come in.

Sebastian.

Yes indeed.

James Morey.

Do I have to give permission to everybody.

You have to give permission to every one you think
responsible.

24

Do I have to choose.

You had better be careful whom you choose.

I will be very careful.

We are all very careful.

SCENE VII.

A great many houses are standing.

And some boats.

A great many boats.

Yes a great many boats have not been lost.

Yes a great many boats are useful.

Do you hear them.

I hear about them.

So do we.

It is not necessary to have a saint.

Why not.

Nobody can answer.

Some do.

What do they answer.

They say that they expect repetition.

Some roses which are here look like winter roses. That only means that they are bought Sunday instead of Friday that only means that they are bought Sunday instead of Friday.

ACT V.

SCENE IX.

Did you mean to be astonished.
The servant.
Did she mean to be astonished.
What is Peru.
A republic.
What is engraving.
Commercial.
What is it likely to lead to.
A competence.
Who enjoys food.
A nervous person.
A mother.
No not a mother
A wife.
Yes a wife.

When do they meet very well.

When they believe in what they have in their house.

Was it all made by them.

Not the things they bought.

No certainly not.

Mr. Morton.

How do you do Mr. Morton.

The whole family.

How can you walk about the country.

Quite easily if you don't mind hills.

One gets accustomed to it.

Why is there a difference between South America and North America.

There is no difference he meant to go there.

After all he was very pleased.

Certainly he was and the results were good.

Excellent.

Mr. Clement.

He went away.

Did he.

Yes and I need a dry climate.

Do you.

I am very well content where I am.

And do you mean to stay.

No I think not.

But you did like Peru.

Very much.

MEXICO

PART II.

Loud voices heard by me.

Did we come back.

All the time that we were saying clouds moon they were feasting.

Rice and everything.

Mr. Gentian.

What are the rest.

I don't know.

There are plenty of early dates. Do dates grow in Mexico. They do somewhere. Not the edible kind. No not the edible kind.

Mr. Hawthorne.

What are the changes.

There are very many of them in some states.

Do you see that.

You mean the house.

Yes I mean that house there.

Yes I see it very well.

In the midst of plenty of separation there is always some one having lawns. Do you like lawns. Of course I do.

There is plenty of time.

In that case let us go quietly.

Yes we will go to see one another.

Another.

Not that today.

By this time we are very weak. Strict. Yes strict. There are a great many calls. Yes there are for that matter.

Many of us have places.

There are said to be five thousand oats eaten daily.

Yes there.

We have no occasion to admit phrases.

We do not admit that thing.
Why not.
Because we have a feeling.
Do be told about a fire.

SCENE II.

Change again. We do not change again.

Easily careful. Say the words. Easily careful to-day.

Martha. Come in.

All the time of merchant marine is taken up with wood. A great deal of wood and then there is no dissatisfaction none at all.

Pearl. What did you say.

The time to suggest winter is when you are very happy. Winter is so pleasant.

I understand advertisements.

All the time.

SCENE III.

That's a very good scene.

Yes sir.

If you want to be respectable address me as sir.

I am very fond of yes sir.

Mildred. Mildred is your name isn't it.

I do not mind anything very much.

Millicent Millicent is your name is it not.

Yes.

I do not wish to make anything too short.

I will make it as long as you wish.

Will you.

Yes.

Dear you are so kind.

Kind you don't like that kind.

Yes I do.

Horace. Have you every heard of Fernville.

Yes indeed it is in the country.

West of Edite.

Yes.

Oh yes.

There was resemblance.

Wasn't there.

Yes indeed there was.

Many flowers. Are there many flowers.

We have a great many.

Tall boys are fourteen.

Or sixteen.

We saw that and it was not a mistake to connect them with feeling pears so that they might know that they could answer very well. They were perfectly satisfactory. Millicent Millicent Foster.

I do believe I find Captain Foster more interesting.

There is no mistake to be made attacks are spoken of and well spoken of and hesitation is not blameable. No one can say that Catholics are proud.

I do not wish to discuss the matter here.

Miss Millicent Wynne.

Why do you sell your name so.

I do not.

Of course you do.

You mean to.

You ask every one about a train.

We were ashamed about the train.

Were you.

Yes we had reason to be.

I can understand. You can understand everything.

A Spanish lesson.

Begin now.

By leaving the room.

No by mentioning why you ave been hesitating.

I have not been hesitating and besides I wish to learn English.

Do you.

Yes.

To read.

To read.

But you read very well.

This cannot be said.

You mean we admire you.

You can do so.

Were they ashamed of their water.

Nobody has any water.
This is what they told us.
Mexico.

SCENE II.

Mexico tide water. I meant not to spell it so.

Mexico tied water.

Mexico border.

I love the letters m and o.

Mr. Gilbert. I do not know that child.

He speaks to you.

Yes he does.

And what does he say.

He asks me what I bequeath to the English.

Does he.

Mrs. Nettie Silk. Have a good time.

We will.

When you say that you pass this way.

You do naturally.

Why don't you return my books.

Do you want them.

Not just a present. You can lend them.

All of them.

Yes all of them.

Thank you so much.

Mrs. William Lane. We found that house.

Yes and we have been accepted.

For what.

For always.

Oh you don't mean to say you won't change your mind.

William will.

So he will.

Yes sir.

The rest of the day.

He wrote about it.

Do you believe him.

I do.

Very well.

Very well.

It doesn't make any difference.

It doesn't make any difference.

Do remember it any way.

Yes I will.

Can I trust you.

Yes Madame.

We will go away.

There is a way.

I know the way.

I know that way.

Yes I know that way anyway.

Don't mean it.

You don't mean it.

Yes sir.

What's the matter.

Bouncing barley I learn it quickly.

All about corn-meal.

This was so curious we thought she had added an egg.

Herbert Guilbert. This is the name. We are pleased with everything. We like birds and curves and I do not mind saying that we like presents.

We are so disappointed.

About what.

About the iron of course.

Mrs. Henry. Do come to see me at my hotel.

I don't think we will.

Good-night.

The light did come up.

At midnight.

No a little after.

We thought it was not difficult.

A little more difficult.

John Beede. I made a mistake.

Harry Shirley. Leaves and leaves of grass and trees.

Oh yes.

In this the way to begin.

Another page. Does she hear me. Does she hear you what.

Turn the page.

Not if you don't do it.

Oh yes.

Alphonse Nester. What's his name.

Didn't you hear it. It came everywhere.

So it did.

A great many people were blamed.

A great many people were blamed.

Robert Nestor. I have heard of him.

Of course you have.

Be careful.

Be very careful.

There is no danger.

There is no danger.

Not to me.

Not for me.

Oh yes.

Say it.

I've said it.

We can say.

Yes.

Tell the young king not to bother.

What do you mean by young king.

I mean that I am willing.

To do what.

To say everything.

He should not have told him.

Well he told Mr. Doux.

Did he.

Of course he did.

I say stop and think.

I say that.

No I don't change it.

Do you like repetition.

Yes I like repetition.

ACT III.

Don't please me with Mexico.

Mr. and Mrs. Bing. They had a book. Yes Miss.

Mr. and Mrs. Guilbert. I mention that name.

Of course you do.

Of course you do to me.

Don't cry.

This is the end of the day. Tomorrow we will leave early. We meet everybody. Some all well fed. Will we be. Well I guess yes. It's foolish to be so abstemious. Are they really. I haven't noticed it.

Mexico.

When you come to choose dishes you should remember that they cure the ham themselves that is smoke it.

Oh yes.

So you should be careful in cooking the fat.

You mean on the island.

She was right. Not about the whole. She knows nothing. Well then why ask her about wood.

In their country they celebrate Sunday.

God bless us I say God bless us all day and all night too.

Do not mention it to me.

When this you see remember me.

I wonder if there is a mistake.

Horace Lewis I can't imagine such a name.

Horace. It is my name.

A great many people are there.

Who says it.

The woods the poor man's overcoat.

We can pronounce everything.

An old man works harder to be eating than a rich one.

Come to me mother.

Don Jose. Have you sold the dog.

Not at all I gave it away.

Don Jose. Where is your dog.

It is in the town.

Don Nicholai. How do you pronounce my name.

So as to go with sow.

That means to sit down.

That means a pig.

Not in this country.

Donna Pilar. Is that cheese.

Yes it's very good cheese.

How do you prepare it.

With cognac.

You mean brandy.

One might not call it wine.

Mrs. Gilbert. I will not insult them again.

Why on account of the lunch they gave you.

No.

Do you know Mr. Bell.

Mr. Henry Bell.

No Mr. Paul Coles Bell.

Oh yes. He teaches English.

Certainly he does.

I would like to teach Spanish.

So would I.

Don Miguel. I believe in a man and wife.

So do I.

And in many children.
And in a new post-office.
We have no opinion about that.

Do please me.

And the sunshine.

Tomorrow.

We hope so.

We have every reason to expect it.

But we may be disappointed.

Peggy Chambers. She went away.

Did she go away.

She deceived him.

How.

She was not educated.

You mean not well educated.

She was not educated to travel.

Does it take an education to travel.

It does if you wish to take part in the conversation.

Bird never took part in the conversation.

54

You are greatly mistaken.
Mark Baldwin. What is your name.
Australia. Did you mention Australia.
Oh yes you mentioned Australia.
We believe in Mexico.

Mexico.

Come to see me in Mexico.

I don't believe in waiting and eating.

That's what we said.

Mark Guilbert. How often I have mentioned his name.

Lindo Bell. I have not mentioned his name before.

Oh yes you have.

Charles Pleyell. This is a name we all know.

My pen is poor my ink is pale my hand shakes like a little dog's tail.

Dorothy Palmer. Where is Ibizza.

Frank Jenny. I do not believe that he is home.

At home.

Yes at his home.

I do not believe that he's out.

Mark Guilbert. He is a young man.

We know three on the island.

Mark, Allan and their mother.

That is not what I meant when I said that she looked American.

I don't quite understand what I have done.

Wintering and rain it is not raining. It rains every day. Oh yes it makes the wood wet. We prefer it so. Thank you you will come to lunch. At what hour. One o'clock. John Russel. If there is a Mallorcan name if Mallorca gave the missionary who converted the California settlers if the Mallorcans have a little town of their own near New York then we will believe in Spanish influence in Mexico. The Spaniards are not liked in Mexico.

John and Maria Serra.

Foundations

The middle of the day. Why do you not come in the day time. You mean to listen. No I don't mean to listen.

58

This is very well said.

Dorothy Palmer Come in and rest.

We are coming in.

A great deal.

A great many mistakes.

Maria Serra. I understand you wish to show me what you have.

Yes.

Will you come tomorrow.

Tomorrow would suit me better.

Or today.

Today would suit me.

Would you be disappointed if Fernando Orro only sang twice.

Of course not.

You mean you would be willing to change your mind.

Of course.

Yes that's it.

Of course a great many people are there and they do not mean to say anything.

You mean praiseworthy.
Yes be glad to meet me.
Yes a diamond.
All the way to come.
Home.

Mexico begins here.

You relieve here.

Here we have star-fish. You mean little ones. Yes little ones.

Mark Gilbert. I wish to tell you about mines.

Yes.

Or would you prefer to hear there were meteors.

I would surely prefer to hear there were meteors.

Any one can refer to it.

So they can.

In the meantime the wind this evening is not nearly in that locality.

Do you think one can say that.

No perhaps not.

Mrs. Penfold. Mrs. Penfold sees no one.

The act of coming is pitiful.

Butter is pitiful.

All of it is enough.

She said it is pleasanter now when there is enough
so that there can be a change.

Mr. and Mrs. Leland Paul.

Do you know that name. Do you know being
called Mr. Paul. Do you hear me telling you that a
great many people hear opera.

A great many soldiers in the streets.

This means that there is wood to prevent traffic.

Not plenty of wood oh no.

Dear Mrs. Amos.

I letter this B because it is very dangerous.

A great many dogs are very dangerous too.

Do you mind. Lilie do you mind.

Yes I do mind.

John Quilly. Do you recollect him.

You mean the color.

Or the effect.

Why yes of course they were beautiful.

So they were.

Will we get some more Tuesday.

I rather guess yes.

A great many.

As many as we can.

All of that one kind.

Yes.

Neglected.

Who has neglected Chinese lillies.

Nobody has. They grow so profusely that there is no necessity to cultivate them.

But the season is so short.

Yes but the wild ones have a finer quality than the others.

SCENE IV.

I said that we were delighted.

If they were blue flowers and grew where chalk is they would be blue.

Clay makes them dark.

Stones make them purple and blue.

This is the color described by the time.

We were not disappointed.

Indeed no.

John Quilly. Why do you rest.

We were so disappointed in the electricity. Of course it was not our fault.

John Quilly. John Quilly John Quilly my babe baby is prettier than ever John Quillys are.

So they selected to do it in two hours.

I can do it in one hour.

I have known it to be done in five hours and a half.

SCENE V.

Have you been relieved.

I should not have mentioned it in the other book.

Oh it doesn't make any difference.

You mean it doesn't matter.

Yes that is what I wished to say.

You have said you believe in delay.

Everybody believes in delay.

Don't annoy me.

ACT VI.

SCENE I.

This is the end. Do you remember the sixth act. I do. It always interested me.

Milly. I thought so.

You mean you thought of a collection

Mrs. Penfold. Mr. Penfold.

Mr. Lindo Howard. I will not be able to be well. I will explain to Harold.

This is what he said.

Mexico is never a disappointment.

Goats. Goats are Western. You mean in excuses. No of course not in feathering.

I do not use that word.

I was so pleased with Mr. and Mrs. Penfold's voices.

Before to-day.

You mean that as a question.

Tito Ruffo.

Tito Ruffo yes.

SCENE II.

Tito Ruffo. No.

That's the way they say it.

They said I like to be separated.

Do you really mean that.

Really and truly.

Mr. Crowell. How do you pronounce it.

We call it well.

Do you mean to say that that is the way you pronounce it.

Yes are you surprised.

Of course I am surprised.

Do you never read the papers.

Not in the morning or evening.

You mean on account of bad news.

No I like flags.

SCENE III.

Alright Mexico.

We did not call for Peppe. This is short for Joseph.

We did not call Pablo.

We did not call Peppe.

We did not have the pleasure of hearing Rigoletto.

William King. Are you pleased with everything.

Certainly I am the news is good.

Marcelle Helen. How do you do I have been in a bombardment.

So you have.

And you were evacuated.

We did not leave our village.

We asked the consul to tell us what he thought.

He said that there was nothing to fear.

Nothing at all.

So he said.

Very well today.

Oh yes the wind.

70

SCENE IV.

I do not make a mistake.

Oh yes indeed.

My mother.

You mean your mother.

I mean to say that I think the government should send her to her home.

We will see.

GREEN INTEGER
Pataphysics and Pedantry

Edited by Per Bregne
Douglas Messerli, *Publisher*

Essays, Manifestos, Statements, Speeches, Maxims,
Epistles, Diaristic Notes, Narratives, Natural Histories,
Poems, Plays, Performances, Ramblings, Revelations
and all such ephemera as may appear necessary
to bring society into a slight tremolo of confusion
and fright at least.

*

GREEN INTEGER BOOKS

Seven Visions Sergei Paradjanov [1998]
Ghost Image Hervé Guibert [1998]
Ballets Without Music, Without Dancers, Without Anything [1999]
Louis-Ferdinand Céline [1999]
On Overgrown Paths Knut Hamsun [1999]
Poems Sappho [1999]
Metropolis Antonio Porta [1999]
Hell Has No Limits José Donoso [1999]
Theoretical Objects Nick Piombino [1999]
Art *Poetic'* Olivier Cadiot [1999]
Fugitive Suns: Selected Poetry Andrée Chedid [1999]
Suicide Circus: Selected Poems
Alexei Kruchenykh [1999]
Mexico. A Play Gertrude Stein [1999]

BOOKS FORTHCOMING FROM GREEN INTEGER

Islands and Other Essays Jean Grenier
Operatics Michel Leiris
My Tired Father Gellu Naum
Manifestos/Manifest Vicente Huidobro
The Doll and *The Doll at Play* Hans Bellmer
[with poetry by Paul Éluard]
Water from a Bucket Charles Henri Ford
What Is Man? Mark Twain
American Notes Charles Dickens
To Do: A Book of Alphabets and Birthdays Gertrude Stein
Letters from Hanusse Joshua Haigh
[edited by Douglas Messerli]